Solar Ethics

Don Cupitt

Solar Ethics

SCM PRESS LTD

0 334 026180

Second Impression 2005

First Published 1995
by SCM Press Ltd
9–17 St Albans Place, London N1 0NX

Printed in Great Britain by
Lightning Source Inc

For the members of Sea of Faith

Contents

Introduction   1

1   The Trouble with Moral Philosophy   6
2   Morality, Ethics and Solar Ethics   10
3   Into the Sun   18
4   Metaphysics and Ethics   23
5   The Fact-Value Split   29
6   Inside Out   36
7   Becoming Objective   41
8   Nihilism and Solarity   49
9   Solarity and Mortality   54
10 Thinking the World of Him   57
11 The Way of No Way   60
12 Levity   65

Further Reading   69

Index   70

Introduction

Early in 1995, just as I was beginning to write this little book, Christopher Bucklow sent me some reproductions of his solar portraits through the post. He is an art historian working part-time at the Victoria and Albert Museum in London, and also a practising artist who since 1993 has been making large photoworks. He explains: 'My pictures are life-size, and each of the "cells" of light is a photograph of the sun's disc. There are 25,000 suns in each silhouette. The blue is the blue of the sky.'

How, I wondered, does he get so many suns side-by-side? The answer turns out to be very simple: he makes a multiple pinhole camera. Each pinhole prints on to the film a perfect little image of the sun, and there are thousands of pinholes, all set within a silhouette of the subject of the picture. Twenty-five thousand, because that is the approximate number of days in the traditional human life-span of seventy years.

Christopher Bucklow's images have been exhibited recently in New York and London. I was pleased by the parallel with some recent themes in my own work, and very pleased also to hear that Chris Bucklow has joined Sea of Faith. It is good to be able to have one of his pictures on the cover of this book.

In philosophical terms, solar ethics is a form of ethical expressivism or emotivism, and should be read against the background of the 'expressionist' philosophy that I have been trying to develop since 1990. In December 1994 I was summarizing what I optimistically described as being my 'final position' in the formula: 'energetic Spinozism, solar ethics, poetical theology'.

The phrase 'energetic Spinozism' labels a thoroughgoing naturalistic vision of the world and of our human life. The world is seen as a self-renewing, endlessly outpouring flux of scattering energies-read-as-signs. Everything is contingent, and the whole is outsideless.

This philosophy was spelled out in *After All* and *The Last Philosophy*. With it belongs the solar ethics here described, the human self being seen as a miniature counterpart of the world. It too burns, pours out and passes away. We should burn brightly, all out.

As for 'the poetical theology', the phrase comes originally from a quotation embedded in Augustine's *City of God*, Book VI. There the late-Roman writer Varro distinguishes between the philosophical theology, which is the truth as known by the philosophers and taught by them in their schools; the civil theology, which is the State religion and is embodied in the annual round of festivals observed in the temple; and the poetical theology, which is the religion taught by poets like Homer and Ovid as they retell the old myths about the gods. There are thus three sorts of religious truth — philosophical, political and imaginative — and it is not surprising that since the Renaissance there has been an irregular line of writers who have taken up the idea of a poetical theology. The old Christian epic doctrine-system cannot nowadays be thought to be dogmatically true, in the 'realistic' sense; but it might come to be seen as poetically true, and by being retold could perhaps gain a new lease of life.

That is by the way. Here we are concerned, not with the poetical theology, but with solar ethics. I am using the word ethics, not in the sense of a moral code, nor even quite in the sense of a 'position' in moral philosophy, but in the old-fashioned sense of a way of living or stance in life which will lead to the highest happiness there is to be had. An ethic is a doctrine of the good life: it teaches a way of life by following which we can attain the highest Good, beatitude.

As I was writing I had again to read and lecture about Martin Buber's *I and Thou* (1923). I realized how sharply my point of view differs from his. Buber distinguishes between two 'primary words', or ways of relating oneself to things, which he calls I–It and I–Thou. Then he grounds his ethic exclusively in the latter, the I–Thou relation. His style of thinking is rather Kantian, but he also resembles other Jewish thinkers such as Emmanuel Levinas in the way he derives the unconditional and sacred character of moral obligation from the mysterious and unmasterable *otherness* with which another person confronts me.

So Buber isolates and clarifies the ethical by making a series of distinctions — between the impersonal and the personal, between the ethical and the non-ethical, and between myself and the Other who confronts me. And I find myself wanting to undercut or dissolve away all three of these distinctions. There isn't, for me, any separate impersonal realm, or anything quite non-ethical. Like Nietzsche, I find valuation to be ubiquitous both in language and in our sense-experience; and like many other religious naturalists I teach a way to happiness, not by giving the human self a special metaphysical status and delivering it from the world, but rather by melting it down into the flux of the world. So the self is not anything numinous, and it does not transcend the flux of phenomena. On the contrary, the self is large, loose-knit and spreading, and thoroughly woven into the world. When you wake in the morning, you don't identify yourself in yourself, as a unique and sovereign spirit: you identify yourself *through* your familiar surroundings, your partner, the day's duties, and your resuming life. In my jargon, you identify yourself through your 'objectivity'; that is, your world.

So I take the ethical very far back, prior to the distinction between I and Thou. I ground the ethical in the self's relation to its own objectivity, its life-world, the focussed, situated and enacted life through which it identifies itself, and into

3

which it continually pours itself out. Consider the way in which I may speak of something as being 'the apple of my eye': the idiom implies that what I love most is so close to me that it is both me and not me — my very life, the apple of my eye, that which I *think the world* of. In short, the beloved object blurs the distinction between the self and the world.

So the ground of the ethical here is the self's relation to its own objectivity, its expressed life in its life-world. Trying to be as naturalistic as possible, I am going as far as I can towards simply equating the ethical with life's own spontaneous and joyful affirmation of itself — life's solar self-outpouring. I am also using the language of solarity to try to push you into accepting that the purest affirmation of life is also a thoroughgoing acceptance of transience and death. I have to push the language hard in order to create a certain literary effect, namely the unity of living and dying that is eternal life. The text is intended to create a bit of the happiness it describes.

What people speak of vaguely and hopefully as 'the meaning of life' — life's supreme End, telos, goal or 'point' — is not something very far away, but something so close to us and so simple that we miss it. I have to look for ways of writing, and for images, that will show it up. Or perhaps bring it out, like the Sun.

As once or twice before, I have to thank various students for contributing criticisms and suggestions when they heard this material delivered as lectures. They include Michael Hunn, Rachel Muers and Eliot Shrimpton. Thanks are once again due to Linda Allen for word-processing, and to Petra Green and Hugh Rayment-Pickard for help with the proofs.

Even in my case a book may be two years in the making from conception to publication, and during that time it may have borne several titles. *Taking Leave of God*, for example, was written to the title, *The Autonomy of Religion*. *The Last Philosophy* was at first *Felicific Philosophy*, and later, *Easy, Going*. This present book's ghostly title is *Good Show*, and while writing it I have been haunted by the slightly archaic use of *brave* in phrases like 'a brave sight'. In most cases, discarded titles are slipped somewhere into the text to ensure that they are not wholly lost, and so it has happened in this case too.

D.C.
Cambridge, June 1995

The Trouble with Moral Philosophy

'Solar ethics' will be an attempt to make a fresh start in moral philosophy; and it should not be difficult to establish the claim that a fresh start is needed.

For consider: modern society is repeatedly swept by waves of moral anxiety — about crime and social disorder, about 'standards' in the media and in public life, about the perceived decline of moral institutions such as marriage and the family, about the intractable and often violent moral disagreements that nowadays surround almost all matters of life and death, about our treatment of animals or the environment, and so on and on. When a moral panic is at its height there is much handwringing, and much nostalgia for a supposedly simpler past when the rules were clearer and folk for the most part *abided* by them. People seize gratefully upon the suggestion that all would be well with us if we would but return to Tradition. They may forget that the value of Tradition can easily be tested by looking at the many small communities of people in our cities who haven't yet lost touch with it. These communities mostly come from the Middle East and from Asia. They cling determinedly to their ancestral languages, their social structure, their customs, beliefs and values. But many or most of them lack the technical and social skills that would enable them to play a full part in modern life, so that they are caught in a sad circle. They cling to Tradition and its values, because it alone can console them for the poverty and exclusion — that their clinging to it is also, sadly, causing them. If we are thinking seriously of going back to Tradition, we should look at the ghettos and count the cost.

Tradition is now way beyond any possibility of revival or recovery; but (you may suggest) there is one obvious alternative to it. Moral philosophy, founded by Socrates, is arguably the oldest and grandest 'academic' subject (its only serious rival being cosmology, which much concerned the philosophers who preceded Socrates). The literature of moral philosophy and ethics is huge, and to this day hundreds — maybe thousands — of people are employed in teaching it. Yet this great tradition remains curiously dim and ineffectual, unconsulted by journalists and unknown to the public. It is felt to be boring: it makes little or no impact. Only a handful of writers from the great tradition are still of any real interest to us, and only now and again does a modern writer such as Alasdair MacIntyre write about them in a way that briefly succeeds in attracting public attention.

Why has moral philosophy failed — or, why is it failing? Why aren't people interested in it? Because, we will reply, it has been too protective of the received moral order, and in its own curious way almost as traditionalist as Tradition itself. It has sought to *justify* morality, clinging to moral realism or objectivism long after that belief had become manifestly untenable. Moral philosophers have been the dogmatic theologians of morality, endlessly trying to postpone a long-overdue revolution within their own subject. Too often, in ethics as in theology, the tradition is studied and commented upon not because it is interesting but merely because it is there, as the syllabus is studied merely because it is the syllabus. Amazingly, moral philosophy was the last subject of all to become truly critical, in the work of writers like Nietzsche and Foucault. That is very late; and it is arguable that much of English-language moral philosophy has still not absorbed their legacy.

What went wrong? At the beginning of this century, reacting against Idealism, Bertrand Russell and G.E. Moore attempted to revive Realism — a realism of sense-data and, in Moore's case, also a form of moral realism: in moral experience one directly intuited the presence of non-natural moral qualities. This bizarre doctrine somehow appealed to the popular feeling that realism is 'commonsense' and occupies the high ground; and so it has remained influential for generations. People felt that you had a moral duty to try to find arguments for moral objectivism or realism; and as for emotivism, it was regarded as the last refuge to which you might find yourself being reluctantly driven, but it was not a position that anyone in their right mind would embrace gladly and in good conscience. Even otherwise robust characters like Russell and Ayer felt they must put on a show of being rather apologetic about being unable to do much better than endorse some form of emotivism in ethics.

Solar ethics is quite different. It makes no bones about being (in traditional terms) a form of emotivism or expressivism. But in order to escape from that wretched high-ground problem we shall be turning many things upside-down and inside-out — and not making any apology at all for doing so. Like theologians, philosophers have got to give up being lackeys of the established order.

So, if you agree that Tradition has failed, and that moral philosophy as we have been doing it has been addressing itself to all the wrong questions; and if you further agree that we need a moral philosophy better fitted to our cosmology and our culture — then you may be ready for solar ethics. The Sun sees no reason at all to apologize for making such an exhibition of itself all the time; it simply is its own outpouring self-expression. It puts on a good show. It has no 'inwardness'; that is, it is not inwardly subject to something unseen that is authoritative over it. It does not experience the moral order as being something distinct from itself and its own activity. It is not *driven*, either by anxiety or by resentment: it is purely and only affirmative. It coincides completely with its own joyous, headlong process of self-exteriorization — and what's wrong with that? A powerful moral need nowadays drives people to seek just such an ethic of self-declaration. They want publicity, they want to demonstrate; they want to come out of the closet and into the open. I think they are right. The public realm is the only real world, and public-ization is real-ization, both for our values and for our selves. Yes, why *shouldn't* we go on a moral spending-spree, burning up not merely our money but our selves?

The older tradition, the great tradition that prevailed at least from Augustine to Kierkegaard, used to seek moral and religious Truth by a flight to the interior. The movement was always inwards, from society to solitude, from expression to recollection, and from outer appearance to inner reality. Perhaps such a turn inwards made sense in a period when people believed that another world was more real than this world. But not now: so here we reverse the movement, setting out instead a solar ethic of uninhibited self-publication. I say flatly that there is no inner space within the self through which we have access to another world more real than this one, and indeed there simply isn't any other world than this one, the common public world that is generated by our expressions and our symbolic exchanges. We do, we must, *come out* to live.

Do you see what is emerging? Everything is immanent, everything comes down to one level. There is no transcendent moral order, there is no inner world within the self, and there is no other sphere of action but this common world of ours. There is nothing left for ethics to be but that we should love life and pour out our hearts — and that is emotivism, or solar ethics. As the man says, 'You are the light of the world' (Matthew 5.14). For solar ethics is a version of Christian ethics, if one may say so.

9

2

Morality, Ethics and Solar Ethics

Even after centuries of discussion, we have still not managed to settle upon any very clear distinction between the scope and the use of the words *morality* and *ethics*. But for our present purpose we do need to draw a few clear lines, between morality, an ethic, ethics and solar ethics.

In order first to define *morality* we do best to begin from the very ancient metaphor of the social world as being like a market. In the marketplace people are moving about, busy with a great variety of acts of exchange. They are bartering, trading, making deals, swapping ideas and arguments, giving undertakings and making contracts. For the market to prosper, and to keep disputes under control, it is in everyone's interest that there should be generally-recognized conventions defining what is to count as fair dealing — what in the tradition stemming from Aristotle is called distributive and commutative justice. So the concern of morality is with securing agreement upon a code of rules governing acts of exchange in some area of human activity.

The market metaphor has proved very powerful and durable; so much so that even today there remains a large overlap between the vocabulary of morality and the vocabulary of business and finance. Indeed, for business-minded people on the political Right, the moral realm is also the economic realm. One thinks of fair shares, fair dealing and fair trade, of straightness, rightness and squareness, of equity, bonds, debt, credit and contracts; of values, obligations and promises. To a remarkable degree the moral order is modelled upon the economic order, moral freedom being closely related to free enterprise and consumer choice, and both realms being constructed as networks of carefully-balanced rights and duties. We should consider the way financial people use words like *owe, pay, payment, due* and *honour*.

Morality as a conventionally-agreed code of practice generates a complex social network of moral relationships; and in traditional societies there was naturally enough a cosmic standard or god of Justice. When at the Enlightenment traditional ways of thinking began to pass away, many people supposed that it was the job of philosophy to step into the breach and provide a foundational justification for morality to replace its now-tarnished supernatural and cosmic backing. But why is this necessary? Surely all human social goings-on tend to become highly rule-governed just by custom and practice? No external lawgiver is required; the rules simply evolve. Obvious examples are the playground games of children, the grammar of languages and the rituals by which (for example) marriages are made. In such cases the rules may very often come to be thought of as sacrosanct; but we do not seriously suppose that they need any deep supernatural or philosophical justification.

So to a modern eye, and in a time of rapid moral change, the renegotiation of the rules of morality looks like a straightforwardly political task. Through public debate one tries to obtain and establish an agreed code of practice, backed where necessary by sanctions. And philosophy nowadays does not need to say very much more about moral codes than that.

Morality, for the most part, can be left to look after itself. Where in any particular sphere of life rules of practice are needed, people can be relied upon to evolve them. So long as the rules are working well people can be relied upon to maintain them, and when they have become redundant or archaic, nothing can revive them and people will let them drop.

By *an ethic* I mean something very different; something that since the early 1970s has come to be called a lifestyle. The social world is now pictured, not as being like a marketplace, but as a theatre or pageant, a scene or show, a stage on which people are playing a variety of different roles. This metaphor is probably as ancient, or almost as ancient, as the market metaphor, but with the emphasis now being upon coming out, demonstration, publication and display.

The two moral worlds have markedly different attitudes to dress. In the marketplace of finance and business, dress tends to be formal. Individual differences are repressed, and instead the emphasis is laid upon the punctilious following of standard procedures. By contrast, where the theatrical metaphors are prominent dress is individual. Personality, style, fashion and appearance come to the fore. For each individual the ethical task is that of finding the right 'scene' for oneself, and then within it a role, a part to play and a style of self-presentation through which one can fully and satisfactorily express oneself and so find one's own form of personal fulfilment and happiness.

During the past half-century the shift from modern to postmodern culture has involved amongst other things a very considerable shift from market to theatre and from rule-morality to lifestyle-morality. We now hear much less about teaching commandments to the young and much more about the ways in which *show*-business celebrities provide *role-models* for the young. Where a hundred years ago (roughly between Matthew Arnold and John Macmurray) people talked of personal integrity, authenticity and sincerity, we now hear people saying that they cannot bear to stay in the closet, living a lie. They want to come out into the open: what is now most highly valued is not so much integrity as expression.

Morality, then, has become aestheticized as lifestyle, and I propose to use the term 'an ethic' to describe a form of self-expression, a manner of coming out. *Ethics* was traditionally a branch of philosophy that sought to answer the question, How should one live? And in particular: What manner of living leads to the highest happiness? Against this backdrop, a post-modern philosophical ethics will take the form of lifestyle-theory. What is it for a human being to come out and put on a good show, and for that matter, what is the best show that can be put on?

By *solar ethics* I mean an ethic or lifestyle of all-out religious expression, the best kind of life that one could hope to live.

I have described the expressionist vision of the world elsewhere. It is a very thoroughgoing form of naturalism. The world is seen as a continuously outpouring, self-renewing stream of dancing energies-read-as-signs, in which our life is wholly immersed. Metaphorically, it is a *broadcast* world, like a firework display. Everything is so *evenly* transient as to create an effect almost of stillness, a very strongly aesthetic effect. Hence the images of the fountain, the Sun, and the slow-motion explosion.

Against such a background, we can see why people's most deeply-felt ethical desire today is for pure expressive freedom. They seek a style of living that completely escapes or disregards, or goes beyond, the traditional binary contrasts in terms of which our culture and our world-view have been constructed in the past.

As has been well said, 'Every ethic dramatizes a metaphysic'. Very well: solar ethics dramatizes expressionism. The metaphor of the Sun is appealing, because in various ways the Sun lives beyond the traditional distinctions.

1. The Sun lives beyond the distinction between living and dying, because the thermonuclear burning by which it lives is also and identically the process by which it is dying. Its whole being is wholly both at once. Because it is utterly heedless, careless and identified with its own pure transience, it cannot

in any way be self-defensive, which makes it a symbol of 'glory', or eternal life — a perfect synthesis of life and death that completely delivers one from self-concern and the fear of death. To achieve a fully religious ethic we must completely give up the notion of life after death, and *also* completely give up the notion of death after life. We learn to fuse the two, living by dying as we go all the time out into expression. Then we'll be able to put on a good show.

2. The Sun lives beyond the distinction between noun and verb, substance and activity, being and doing. In the old scholastic language, it is pure Act. It coincides with its own continuous outpouring. To repeat an adjective used above, the Sun is all-out.

The point is important, because too many of our European languages distinguish too sharply between substance and activity, noun and verb, and so they tend to generate the illusion of non-temporal Being. But all Being is temporal, participial be-ing, like the be-ing of lightning, rain or a symphony. It is a process or performance that occurs or is enacted in time; and so is ethical personhood. We exist in, and only *as*, the performance we are giving and the show we are putting on. We have no being apart from our life. We become ourselves only in passing and in passing away.

3. The Sun lives beyond the distinction between the ideal and the actual, because its self-expressive outpouring is so complete that it is everything it can be or should be. It pours its heart out, it can do no more; it is perfect, because it gives all it's got. You cannot ask for more than that, because there *is* no more.

I say this because we are so accustomed to the thought that the ideal or moral order is always above and ahead of us, always finding that we fall short of the standard it sets, always making us feel inadequate to it. A truly religious ethic will be one that helps us to escape from these wearisome reproaches. And what form will it take? — it must be an expressionist ethic. When we have come fully out into the open and have given all we've got then we shall have, as people rightly say, 'Nothing whatever to reproach yourself about'. Full expression delivers one from the tyranny of the ideal. When I'm utterly emptied, I'm satisfied.

4. The Sun lives beyond the distinction between inner and outer, because it simply is its own process of complete and continual self-outing, self-exteriorization, appearance. The Sun is blessedly free from the outworn and deeply ugly idea that outwardness is vanity, shallowness, playacting. It knows nothing of the old Western notion that inwardness is more real and true and lasting. It has no inwardness, and no inhibition whatever about making a complete exhibition of itself. It simply turns itself inside out; it goes public all over the place. It is its own self-outing.

5. The Sun is utterly indifferent to, and lives beyond, the ever-popular distinction between the good people and the bad, the saved and the lost, the respectable and the dirty. People may distinguish themselves from each other by their different responses to it, but the Sun itself does not discriminate. On the contrary, as the Teacher says, it just shines on all alike indiscriminately (Matthew 5.45).

Tropical, and especially desert, peoples see the Sun as being both Creator and Destroyer. The same pure burning natural energy may bring creation, destruction or both, and in any case the two are always intimately associated with each other. To have the strength to do the one, you need also the courage to do something of the other.

In modern Britain it can seem that we have lost the will to destroy because we have lost the confidence to create, and *vice versa*. But the Sun's furious joyful self-expenditure is both creation and destruction at once.

6. The Sun escapes the distinction between the Way and the End, the journey and the destination. This is an important and difficult point to grasp. In religious language it is sometimes said that Christ is both the Way and the End, and similarly you may suppose that the Sun symbolizes *both* a

certain way of living, *and* the Goal or End to which that way of living may be thought to lead us. But I mean more than that. Where I am now, there is no Beyond; and where you are now, there is no Beyond. All this is all there is. We should see ourselves as living *already at* the End, and therefore we should live in a manner that escapes or overcomes the means/end distinction. We should live expressively, outing ourselves, shining, burning, and going down with all guns blazing.

So much for a very preliminary characterization of solar ethics. Enough to be going on with; and enough to explain what we mean by saying that whereas the Law is concerned to set up, to enact and enforce the distinctions, a religious or 'solar' ethic is an attempt to live beyond the distinctions. The law sets up a clear cosmological and disciplinary framework; but solar ethics bursts out of the old world-view.

There is a further and larger corollary. We live at a time when our outlook is becoming completely immanent or naturalistic. Everybody is beginning to suspect the truth, which is that the supposed 'inner space' of subjectivity was only ever a cultural construct, a manner of speaking. There is no more-real private world inside us. There is no objective moral order. There is no more-Real world above, and no objective order of Reason. Outsidelessly, there is only the solar flux of creation and destruction, the outpouring self-renewing stream of dancing and scattering energies-read-as-signs. And in this context, solar ethics is a religious ethic for the world and for life as we now know it to be. If you wish to live not by Tradition but simply in the truth, solar ethics is for you.

Solar living replaces traditional ideas of Transcendence and self-transcendence, and I am also suggesting that it does more than that. It consummates them. Beyond the distinctions there is a furious solar joy that fulfils older ideas of Transcendence; and in purely expressive living, by solar self-outing, there is a new form of self-transcendence. So, *burn!*

Note

A student, R.M., comments that although I may be right in suggesting that moralities, in the sense of codes of practice, can be left to evolve where and as they are needed, and are not as such of great philosophical concern, there is still a problem about the relation between solar ethics and moralities. As we have so far described it, solar ethics sounds like an ethic for artists, stars, bohemians and holidaymakers; but in the workaday world there must be disciplines, codes of practice and long-term planning. Perhaps I have dismissed moral codes philosophically, and have forgotten that they are nevertheless needed in social and economic life. Even solar people have to conform to some rules.

In discussion, we agreed that in modern Western societies (at their best) it is quite possible for minute regulation in some areas of life to be combined with a considerable degree of expressive freedom in others. Perhaps solarity and morality can coexist without conflict? But there remains a difficulty: how in practice does one combine solar heedlessness and short-termism with the need for at least some long-term planning of *one's own* life?

A critic-friend complains about the ugly word 'self-exteriorization'; why not use the simpler and clearer 'self-expression'? The answer is that the neologism was coined to jolt the reader. In Northern, Protestant cultures a process of internalization, *innerlichierung*, has been going on for centuries. But perhaps it has hit the buffers, and is now clanking into reverse. And perhaps that is a good thing, too.

3

Into the Sun

There is another respect in which the Sun lives beyond the distinctions. From a 'solar' point of view the old issue between theism and atheism is not of prime importance. Instead, solar living involves learning new ideas of the human self, the world and the ways in which they are related.

The old 'platonic' binary contrasts — sense and reason, particular and universal, finite and infinite, contingent and necessary, and so forth — functioned to lift up the human soul a little from the body, and out of the flux of this world. They oriented the soul towards an eternal world in which it would find both intellectual and moral norms to live by in this life, and also hereafter its eternal destiny.

A corollary of the old outlook was a contrast between the immortal soul and the mortal, corruptible human flesh. A certain obsessive dwelling on bodily death and corruption was very common.

The solar point of view completely gives up the contrasts, and gives up the idea that anything is fixed or unchanging. The world is like a fire or a fountain, an outpouring, self-renewing, utterly contingent and outsideless flux of energies-read-as-signs. And we are completely immersed in it. We should cast ourselves joyfully into the flux of existence. We should give, give our all, give out, and give *up*, turning loss into oblation. We should burn, burn away and burn out.

If we are thus wholly immersed in the flux of existence, how does the self get to distinguish itself from the not-self, the environing world, *at all*? To see what happens, look around the room now; look out of the window. Recognize, name *everything*. Empty yourself out over the world through your eyes, as a painter does. Feel how world-energies come welling up and support you, and in return language flows out from you to form, organize, make conscious and embellish the world of your experience. From moment to moment, in our own life-activity, the world pours out and becomes finished and beautiful.

'Ecstatic immanence', then, is an intense and joyous response to the pure flux of existence. One is completely given to the moment in which world-energies emerge, come into Be-ing as they are formed by signs and become bright-lit, conscious, cosmos. One discovers a certain reciprocity, partnership, communion between the self and the world. We are the world's and the world is ours, each outpouring and making the other simultaneously.

Ecstatic immanence crops up sporadically in the mystical tradition and in lyric poetry, both in the West and in the East. But it begins to be seriously democratized only from the 1880s or thereabouts, in the eye of Monet, the solar expressivism of Van Gogh, and the prose of Nietzsche. The reason for this late arrival is obvious: you can begin to live in the solar way and experience ecstatic immanence only *after* you have escaped from the domination of the old contrasts between the sensual and the spiritual, the fleeting and the eternal and so on. For the same reason, I hesitate to call ecstatic immanence a form of 'spirituality', because the concept of a spirituality seems to presuppose the old ugly dualism between your outer and your inner life, and between the carnal and the spiritual.

Solar living, then, starts *after* the end of metaphysics and after the Death of God, and it is therefore relatively unconcerned about the theism/atheism issue. One need not think in such ways. And similarly, those who have learnt how to find eternal happiness in the purely contingent and outsideless flux of life are delivered from the fear of death. It no longer seems in the least unnatural or disgusting.

Happily, people are already changing. In the Anglican poet John Betjeman one sees the old realistic type of religious belief decaying, and producing a phobia about the flesh and death. Maggots chew eyeballs, mouths are filled with clay, and fingerbones stick out of finger-ends. Such is the pathology of the 'old moth-eaten brocade', the type of religion that is now passing away.

A more recent and healthier response to death is illustrated by a very-frequently recurrent dream of 1993. 'I am in a slender and heavily-insulated spacecraft, travelling across the orbits of Venus and Mercury, and then, plunging straight down into the Sun. I am lying down because of the gravity problem, but I can see out a little. The white fury outside grows stronger. Soon it will break in — and I will welcome it. I feel great jubilation at the thought of being utterly consumed, very soon.'

Why the jubilation; and is this a traditionally religious dream? Perhaps it is, for one of the strongest impulses in religion is the desire to become securely lodged in or united with the cosmic Centre. This Centre is always seen as the source of all 'light', or intelligibility. It is an intense concentration of energy and it is the giver of all life. So in the Bible, in ancient Egypt and in Greece there are very strong traditions of solar symbolism, and in both the Old and the New Testaments God is pictured as a consuming fire.

Admittedly, the Sun is only a creature. An encounter with God would be infinitely more terrible than dropping into a mere twenty-million-degree furnace. But in terms of the history of religious symbolism death by plunging into the Sun does seem to be a clear metaphor for union with God. The mystics have indeed spoken of being consumed by fire and of 'dissolving in God' (a Russian phrase). And the metaphor is made all the more attractive by the fact that the Sun's daily course across the sky from sunrise to sunset is everywhere seen also as a metaphor for human life. An old person sitting and watching the sun go down in the evening may very well dream of going down with it, going down into it.

Some years ago an enterprising American was selling space for customers' ashes aboard a promised rocket to be fired one day into the Sun. A possible source for the dream; for people who were willing to buy themselves tickets for such a posthumous journey must have seen union with the Sun as being somehow very close to union with God.

So much for one line of interpretation of the dream. But there is another, for at the time of the dream the dreamer had been reading Bataille, in whose surrealist imagination the Sun is a less friendly object. It is a plucked-out eyeball, a severed human head, a human heart cut from a sacrificial victim and held aloft by an Aztec priest, a bleeding slaughtered bull, a screeching cock and also the rolling delirious sun of Vincent Van Gogh. And not only all that, for Bataille's Sun becomes also an erupting volcano, an anus, a slashed eye and more. It becomes, in short, a lurid symbol of Bataille's 'virulent nihilism'; and the fall into the Sun may be seen as a repetition, a reversal and a finalization of the Fall of Icarus. In which case the fall into the sun would be a fall into final damnation.[1]

So much, then, for the theistic and the atheistic interpretations of the dream of plunging jubilant down into the Sun. But because I have argued that solar living is a new way of living beyond the old distinctions, I don't myself accept either of those interpretations. I think that the dream was just a dream of ecstatic immanence. Fully expressed, and therefore utterly consumed, one passes joyfully away into the flux of things.

Do you see that we are talking about what a pupil/critic of mine once called 'Protestantism squared'? Living by faith, living by self-abandonment, living by expressive self-outpouring, whether from one's heart or through one's eyes. It resembles Protestant faith in that it is a way of escaping from sin, from the weight of the past and the fear of the future, and from defensiveness, by being so emptied out that there is nothing left to be defended.

In a discourse the Buddha speaks of the speed of transience. So fast does everything slip away that it is like the speed of light, the speed of thought. And when one is exposed nakedly to transience one *burns*, like a live coal when a draught blows over it.

Note

[1] On Bataille, see Mark C. Taylor, *Altarity* (Chicago 1987) ch.5; and Nick Land, *The Thirst for Annihilation: Georges Bataille and Virulent Nihilism* (Routledge 1992). Bataille comes closest to solar ethics in *Le Bleu du Ciel*, 1957, translated as *Blue of Noon* (Marion Boyars 1979).

4

Metaphysics and Ethics

In the *Sophist* (263E) Plato writes: 'Thought and speech are the same; the inner dialogue of the soul with itself has been called thought.'

This is very striking. Plato once again shows himself capable of considering some very unplatonic theses.[1] Did he ever trace out the implications of this one? If all our thinking is transacted in our language, then 'the mind' and all our supposed inner life of thought must be a secondary internalization. Words must first be introduced and traded back and forth in the public and interpersonal realm, so that they can get settled and stable patterns of use, before they can enter into our trains of thought. And the private realm of thought therefore cannot be privileged: its scope cannot be greater than the scope of the public realm upon which it draws. Furthermore, what you can think must be limited by the special features of the natural language and the other symbol systems *in* which you think.

All this makes 'the mind' not a metaphysical entity with access to a higher world, but simply a contingent cultural construct. No more than that. Society is logically prior to solitude, and not the reverse; and publicity is prior to privacy. In each case the former is essential, and the latter just an optional extra. Most modern people have rather a lot of inner life; or, at any rate, our established ways of speaking impute a rather active subjective consciousness to people; or, putting it more cautiously still, we have many mentalistic idioms in the language. But whether an inner life of subjective consciousness is actually a good thing, and beneficial to those who possess it (or have it imputed to them) may be doubted. Bronze Age people and perhaps early mediaeval people did very well without it.

There is, however, another and much more radical consequence of Plato's hypothesis. If our thinking life is radically dependent upon language, then knowledge itself and all our awareness of the world is mediated by language. Indeed, for us the world must be always already packed in language. And our many different languages by no means present the world to us shrink-wrapped in transparent clingfilm. Rather, they *encode* it within syntactically-ordered chains of conventional signs.

To avoid misunderstanding, I should say at this point that words and phrases do often have strong feeling-associations that they bring with them and can make conscious or vivid. Suppose I say 'Sydney Opera House'. The phrase, associated as it is with other words — 'white', 'concrete shells, sails' — seems to call up and make conscious a standard iconic visual image, a side view from across the water. So words do indeed, as I've said elsewhere, have the power to fix feels and make them regularly accessible to us. But note that all the detailed features of the feel can be accessed only with the help of *more* words; and to think *about* the Opera House I've got to follow verbal associations. What began by seeming to be a freestanding visual image thus turns out on analysis to be as much formed and assembled by language as is your present visual field. So coherent propositional thought — knowledge, facts — remains radically dependent upon language, and 'mental pictures' are *not* counter-examples.

I do allow, then, that there are more-or-less fragmentary feels linked with words. To that extent, there is mental imagery. But connections and associations *between* feels are, I insist, language-mediated (or, at least, sign-mediated) *in every case*. And this applies even to the case of a rising scale of musical notes. Conventional musical signs — scales, notes, etc. — alone make it possible for you to access the subjective feels of the successive tones. David Hume (*Treatise* I, I, i; Selby-Bigge ed., p.6) made a well-known slip here. His empiricism led him to claim that 'impressions' — sensuous feels — are philosophically prior and foundational. But they are not: they come second. Our linguistic and other signs come first. They scale and structure the flux of our feelings, giving us reliable, repeatable and publicly-checkable access to it. And I am accordingly confident that the words 'Sydney Opera House' will do much the same for you as they do for me — not because I trust visual images, but because we can all trust words. Visual images are merely private, but words are public and accessible to all.

I conclude then that language structures the whole world of experience, and that language also brings along with it all the sensuous feels of things.

To put the point in traditional British empiricist terms, language both *forms* our sense-impressions and gives us a handle on them, and also does *all* the associating of our impressions that builds up our world-view.

How far Plato himself may have pursued the implications of the doctrine that 'thought and speech are the same', we do not know. In the *Republic*, he does say that language is used differently by people who have emerged from the Cave into the different world above. But he seems not to have considered the possibility that in our world people who speak different natural languages, or who speak the same natural language in widely-separated historical epochs, may be thinking very differently and building very different worlds.

But such ideas are familiar today. They emerged in Martin Heidegger's *Introduction to Metaphysics* lecture-course, delivered at Freiburg in 1935. 'Words and language are not wrappings ...', he says, 'It is in language that things first come into being and are' (tr. Ralph Mannheim, Yale UP 1987, p.13). And it is well-known that in the same years Whorf in America, Wittgenstein in Britain and Lacan in France were developing similar ideas.

The ethically-important point that I am stressing is the

logical and philosophical priority of our public and communicative life. We need to get rid of the idea of the superior moral reality and religious value of the inner world of subjectivity. Especially we need to get rid of the idea that when we retire into inwardness and commune with our own consciences, we access a Higher World, a world of moral absolutes and the like. No: *your soul is your role!* Your only real life is your life of communicative action and collaborative world-building with other people. Your life is a process of solar self-exteriorization, going out into expression. So get going! To become somebody you've got to go out into the dissolution of expression.

But now you may protest. Is there something wrong here in the fit between metaphysics and ethics? The ethical doctrine commands you to live as the Sun does, expending yourself in communicative life-giving self-exteriorization; but the metaphysical doctrine says that that is all that any of us can ever do anyway. The ethical doctrine says *Externalize!* The metaphysical doctrine says *Our human life is all self-externalization.* Isn't there some redundancy here? Why urge people to do what you have just proved they are always doing anyway?

The short answer is that most of moral philosophy since Plato has been predicated upon the presumption that human beings start off in a condition of alienation from the Good. People are thought to need authoritative guidance, a disciplinary structure, 'absolutes', laws, restraints, to get them from the bad state in which they all begin to the Better World in which they want to end up. But I am rejecting the presumption of alienation, for a twofold reason: first, we do not have sufficient grounds for believing that there is any Better World elsewhere; and secondly, after Darwin and many other great thinkers of the nineteenth century we have very strong grounds for supposing that this world of our human intercourse is in any case our true and only home.

If then we decline the traditional presumption of

alienation, we will refuse to contrast this life with a better life elsewhere or hereafter. We will give up the idea that the moral realm is a distinct realm from the empirical realm. We won't any longer see morality as an attempt to bring this recalcitrant world of Nature under a foreign jurisdiction. Instead we will embrace a form of ethical naturalism, seeing the moral life as calling upon us to plunge wholeheartedly into the life of this world, exteriorizing ourselves, going out into expression and into the common human enterprise of world-building. Solar ethics is kingdom-ethics, radically expressivist, affirming life and affirming transience, careless of death, burning and burning out. Solar ethics lives like Vincent Van Gogh paints.

The answer to the question about overlapping and seeming redundancy in the relationship between our metaphysics and our ethics, then, is that the very distinction between metaphysics and ethics, between is and ought, between the world of fact and the moral realm, between the actual and the ideal — the feeling that there is a need to draw that distinction is *itself* a symptom of alienation. I am trying to close it, trying to bring about first the concentricity and then the full confusion (or melding together) of the two worlds, so that the world of Becoming, the everyday world of transient appearances is first seen as being itself outsidelessly the only world, and then is joyfully affirmed as being itself *of course also* the world of eternal value into which we hope to pass by dying. In all our action, we die to live.

The relation between the world and the self is asymmetrical. The world empowers you, pouring into you its own Dionysiac flux of upwelling energies; and you in complementary response go out into linguistic expression, into the action and the consciousness which give the world its Apollinian *shine*, its finished dazzling all-human beauty. So the world powers you, and you finish it in such a style that people can say that language calls the world into being. The relationship is two-way because it is simultaneously true in the fleeting instant *both* that the alluring dance of language calls forth the flux of Becoming, *and* that the flux of Becoming powers the dance of language. Outsidelessly, in the fleeting moment, that-we-make-the-world coincides with that-the-world-makes-us.

In this ubiquitous moment of Be-ing a number of slogans coincide, and I have explained them elsewhere: cosmic humanism, world-mysticism, ecstatic immanence, solar ethics. The moment is our version of the 'initial singularity'. It is so intense that it generates a great deal of writing. And here is another slogan or technical term: *levity*, signifying both lightness and joy. For just as it is liberating and joyful to find oneself a beliefless Christian who is still a Christian (and all the more so, indeed) even after having shed all the ragged and rusty old burden of dead doctrinal beliefs, so too it is joyful to find oneself absorbed in love of the human world after having got rid of the old belief in a non-natural moral order and moral code, and it is also joyful to have shed, or to have reached the end of, Western metaphysics.

Levity? — the joke is that the end of Western thought should turn out to be not a condition of maximal accumulation and totalization, like a Baroque palace or like the closing chords of a Romantic symphony, but rather, a condition of extreme lightness — and therefore, joy.

Note

[1] On platonism and language, A.T. comments that in Plato's own text the progress of the soul is achieved not by withdrawal into solitude and recollection, but through dialogue, dialectic, conversation. And something of the kind may still be said of Augustine himself (*Confessions* IX, x), who achieves his highest flight of mystical ecstasy not in solitude, but while he is in conversation with his mother Monica at the window of the house in Ostia.

5

The Fact-Value Split

The shortest way to a clear view of the state of ethics in our culture is by a sketch of the history of the fact-value distinction.

In the earliest times and until late in the Bronze Age, there was no clear separation between the world where the gods lived and the world in which human beings lived. The invisible heavenly world of eternal values and the visible world of transient fact had simply not yet become sharply distinguished from each other. On the contrary, the gods were part of the cosmos, and this world was regarded as having been built by them not just for us but also for *themselves* to live in. (So conservative is religion that there are 'houses of God' on earth to this day!) Religion commonly worked to sacralize both the social order and the cosmic order, annually returning everything into the primal perfection that the gods had established in the beginning.

The peculiar good fortune of Bronze Age life lay in the fact that the future had not been invented, and did not yet exist. Instead, time was cyclical, continually reconnecting society with its sacred Origin. The annual round of feasts curved back into the Beginning, and then returned refreshed and renewed into the present. So where we in our culture put the future, they put simply the regular repristination of the present, and they were thus blessedly without the ideas of anxiety, freedom, sin, history, and the progressive decline and decay of the world. There wasn't yet a fact-value split: everything was, and could be kept, just as it should be. Even in death, one didn't leave the world but merely passed over into permanent union with it. Sealed into the cosmos, in final immanence.

It did not last: in the Iron Age, around or just before the times of Plato, Mahavira and the Buddha, a more pessimistic outlook developed. The world of the gods, of timeless values and intelligible Forms, became invisible and withdrew, henceforth being sharply contrasted with the lower world of changing and deceitful appearances. Gradually it came to be universally believed that all of our human life is radically unsatisfactory. Some disaster has occurred, as a result of which we find ourselves born into the wrong world and alienated from our true Home. The old ritual renewal of everything in a festival of creation and enthronement no longer happens. The Good is now found to be completely absent from this world, and human life perforce becomes a pilgrimage, a Long March in search of deliverance, and therewith also a strenuous task of self-purification. A series of binary contrasts becomes fixed in the language, every one of them stressing the disjunction between the two worlds and the state of radical alienation in which we poor humans consequently find ourselves: description and evaluation, indicative and imperative, is and ought, facts and values, the actual and the ideal, time and eternity, the relative and the absolute, the changing and the unchanging, phenomena and noumena, sensuousness and Reason, body and soul, flesh and spirit, and so on.

To this day, these contrasts remain embedded in our language. They have worked to make us feel bad about this life, and to produce moral pessimism. People are still influenced by the notion that we are born fallen, exiled in the wrong world. Nothing about us is as it should be. We are so estranged from the Good that it is hard to see how we as we are can ever attain it, or bring it down into this world. We need to be rescued.

Our current moral pessimism, our moral panics and our clamour for moral discipline thus do not show anything very much about the way the world is. What they rather show is the continuing influence upon us of a pessimistic world-view twenty-six centuries old. Plato's version of it associates the Good with what is universal and purely rational; with, that is, pure intelligible Form, exalted above the flux of this fallen world. The Good is both supremely real and supremely rational, so that the work of moral discipline and self-purification by which we seek to transcend ourselves and to attain the Good *coincides with* the philosopher's quest for the supreme object of knowledge.

The Christian version of all this started from the seemingly indefinite postponement of Christ's awaited return in glory to establish the Kingdom of God upon earth. The effect of the delay, so shocking at first, was to defer final salvation either until after death or into the remotest future, and life on earth became a journey through the Wilderness, under the quasi-military discipline of the Church and fortified by her sacraments. 'O turn away mine eyes, lest they behold vanity', chanted the monk, 'And quicken thou me in thy way' (Ps. 119.37 *BCP*). One did not wish to see too much of this world.

It might be thought that the coming of modernity would change all this. Not so: on the contrary, the revolution in natural philosophy that came with Galileo and Descartes was brought about by separating the gaining of knowledge from any work of self-purification, and by stripping value out of the physical world even more thoroughly than had been done before.[1] Modern mathematical physics allows the physical world really to possess only mathematical properties, and aims to comprehend it with all the clarity and distinctness of the mathematician's grasp of truth. So natural science became committed to an ideal of lucid, objective knowledge, and to an ideology of its own religious, political and moral neutrality. The distinction between the worlds of physical fact and of moral value thus became clearer than ever. In brief: the stronger physics gets to be, the more alienated from value we all become.

If the physical world — of which each of us is after all bodily a part — is thus a completely value-free zone, how does morality ever get to impinge upon us human beings at all? Picking up on Cartesian mind-matter dualism, British utilitarianism relocates moral value in the mental realm. The only intrinsically valuable or dis-valuable things are states of consciousness, feelings of pleasure or pain, happiness or misery. The alternative and rationalist view, best stated by Kant, is a kind of ultraplatonism. It denies that even our feelings or inclinations can be moral, saying instead that the only intrinsically good thing is the pure rational Form of the moral agent's intention in acting — 'the good will'. So for the rationalists intrinsic goodness can reside neither in anything physical nor in anything psychological, but only in something noumenal and inaccessible, the rational form of an intention.

All this makes it clear why moral philosophy has failed, or seems to have failed. The philosophers of the Enlightenment thought that a new post-traditional justification for morality was needed but, after Platonism, and especially after the rise of the new mechanistic science, they could not find it in Nature. It seemed that contact with the ethical had to be pushed back deep into human subjectivity. It was typically said either that a psychological state, pleasure, is the only good, or that the pure abstract moral legalism of 'duty for duty's sake' is the only good.

The human being thus became increasingly split between outward and bodily appearance and inward and noumenal or spiritual reality. We are all amphibians, who live in two worlds at once: in Kant's phrase, we are 'phenomenally determined, but noumenally free'. Kierkegaard's man walking in the Deer Park was outwardly just like any other bourgeois citizen, but inwardly related himself to Eternity. Indeed, a sharp contrast between your outer appearance and your inner reality was a sign of merit. Every human being was living a double life, like a spy, or a closet homosexual who cannot come out. We were thought to have a second, secret identity which may not or cannot be declared publicly. And this was, supposedly, an *interesting* condition to be in.

In popular fiction since Kierkegaard this theme of a second or 'closet' identity has been very thoroughly explored. What *is* the secret: a criminal past, a mission as a spy, supernatural powers, a sexual perversion or deviation, noble birth ...? And why can it not be revealed: for reasons of shame, or duty, or loyalty; or might it be a secret that somehow is *logically* unpublishable? Kierkegaard seems to take this last view, for although he writes so much about being 'a spy in Higher Service' and 'under Governance', he is of course also indicating that the believer's second and hidden allegiance is such that it *cannot* be described or communicated directly, but only indirectly. Which is similar to what Kant says about moral freedom: we have to believe in it, but we cannot explain clearly what it is or even how it is possible.

Enough: I am suggesting that the very fact that the great tradition of Western thought about the self and the moral life had reached this shocking position in Kant and Kierkegaard is enough to show that a revolutionary shift in outlook was long overdue. Kierkegaard might retort sharply that the notion that we have a hidden identity, a citizenship elsewhere, comes ultimately from the New Testament (Ephesians 2.19; Hebrews 13.14 etc.). But in those days people ardently hoped and confidently expected to be spectacularly outed, and very soon, by God himself — whereas the Kierkegaardian believer is under a religious imperative to remain in the closet for life, and the Kantian moral agent thinks it philosophically impossible to explain how the same goings-on can be at once free moral action and caused behaviours. Neither Kant nor Kierkegaard can explain clearly how the inner reality of what we are can ever reach full publication. For both of them, we are split and condemned to stay split.

I am saying then that a situation in which people find

themselves (whether for philosophical or religious reasons) forced to live a double life in perpetuity is intolerable. We should have every sympathy with people in sexual or religious minorities who want to come out into the open. Solar or expressionist ethics is all about coming out and putting on a brave show, strutting one's stuff, doing one's thing. It flatly repudiates the whole idea of the superior reality of inwardness and hiddenness. Reversing the late Duke of Wellington, it says: 'Publish and be saved!' We will never be fully at ease with ourselves until we have come out and declared ourselves.

How can this be done, if our philosophical situation is as dire as Kant says it is?

First, we have to overcome the long dominance in our culture of (realistically-understood) mathematical physics. Philosophically-speaking, the ordinary person is correct in assuming that the first world is the ordinary human life-world. It is logically prior; and it is not a mathematician's world, but a talking animal's life-world, coloured up by that animal's interest in life. The space before us, the colours we see, the noises we hear, the odours we scent — these, the traditional 'secondary qualities', have long been thought of as 'subjective': but now we see that they are indeed our own feeling-responses, spread over the life-world to such an extent that our life-world is *exactly* as much our construct as we are its. Pouring ourselves out expressively, we enrich and embellish our world, which in turn enriches and sustains us. Think of your world, your own Other, as your better half: you form it, it nurtures you.

Secondly then, and against this background, we need to acknowledge that so far from the objective world being value-neutral, valuation is on the contrary ubiquitous in it and constitutive of it. I mean that our differential evaluations of and feeling-responses to experience structure the world. Nietzsche, for example, notes:

The extent of moral evaluations: they play a part in almost every sense-impression. Our world is *coloured* by them.

The Will to Power, § 260 (Kaufmann)[2]

And *thirdly*, then, if we approach questions of morality and value inductively we will find that morality doesn't need to be justified, but only to be criticized. Valuations are already implicit in all our experience, all our linguistic usages and practices. Our biological feeling-life and our evaluative life coincide. They are the same. There is always already a moral order, felt in the way we see things and speak about them. But there is very often a strong case for valuing something or someone more highly, speaking of it more kindly, giving it a better name, and so coming to appreciate it more and treat it better. This enriches both the world and us.

As a general ethical maxim, then, it is rational for us to love and to value every aspect of the world and our lives as highly as it consistently compossible (see *The New Christian Ethics*, 1988, [2]1993). To live like that is to live as the sun does, purely affirmatively. We simply avoid giving employment to *ressentiment* and the 'passive' or 'reactive' emotions. It is irrational to devalue any bit of our world, because we thereby also devalue a bit of ourselves.

Which shows that solar ethics, when fully spelled out, will one day provide a philosophical rationale for the religious ecohumanism of the future.

Notes

[1] The originality of Descartes on this point is very well stated by Foucault in a late interview: see Paul Rabinow (ed.), *The Foucault Reader*, Penguin Books 1986, pp.371f.

[2] David Hume makes a similar expressivist point when he says that 'the mind has a great propensity to spread itself on external objects' (*Treatise*, Book I, Part III, XIV; Selby-Bigge ed., p.167).

6

Inside Out

Five years ago, at a party. Someone talking with great animation, enjoying herself. Every bit of her was broadcasting information, radiating messages. Dress, body-language, facial expression, gesticulation, high-speed talk — she was all communication. She was *solar*, and indeed when people are as energetically expressive as that we do speak of them as emitting light, sparkling, shining, radiant, dazzling. The phrase came to me: 'A human being, a fountain of signs'.

Notice that when people are thus shining, absorbed in communicative expression, they are totally unaware of *morality*. They are entirely heedless of any hidden world of standards constraining their behaviour. They are, as one might say, 'ecstatically immanent' in their own expressive activity. They are identical with their own self-outpouring.

The vision of the world that I have called expressionism, or 'energetic Spinozism' is a very thoroughgoing form of naturalism. The world is seen as a continuously outpouring self-renewing stream of energies-read-as-signs. And from that last phrase it follows that we must be the same. In order to make us into sentient, thinking, talking beings, beings with a common world, culture has trained us to feel and read the motion of our own and other people's bodily energies as a motion of signs. Now we can enter into communication with other people, and now too we can read the ambient world. What our communication is made of is perforce also what we, others and the world are made of.

So it is right that in so many systems of thought

anthropology is a miniature version of cosmology. Hence, the images of the fountain, the Sun, the slow-motion explosion and so forth are images both of the cosmos and of the individual human being.

By this route we can hope to reach the most all-round and reflexively complete form of naturalism yet produced, for this text that I am sweating to write and you (I trust) to read is *itself also* a bit of what it says the world is and a human being is. Everywhere there runs the same sort of stuff: one outpouring manifold flux of world-energies-read-as-signs constitutes the world itself, the human person (typified by my talkative partygoer) and this text as it is written or read. The medium is in every way both consonant and concurrent with its own message. And this thought, of our own here-and-now radical immanence in the endless transient outsideless flux of all things, ought suddenly to create in you an effect of eternal happiness. Does it?

According to the excellent saying earlier quoted, 'Every ethic dramatizes a metaphysic'. Then, much as the old monastic way of life dramatized the value-contrast between the world of sense below and the eternal world above, so solar ethics dramatizes the expressionist vision of the world as an outsideless outpouring flux of energies-read-as-signs.

Notice that on this view there is not just one objective Truth of things out-there. On the contrary, the world and the human condition are plastic enough to be capable of various readings. And there is not just One True Morality out there. On the contrary, various perceptions of and responses to the human condition may give rise to various ethics. There can be various moralities, and some of them may be very cruel and strange — sometimes, because the world-view that they are dramatizing is itself cruel and strange.

To grasp what is at stake here, we should set aside for a moment our usual innocent assumption of the morality of morality. Apologists for morality often try to get away with the tacit suggestion that it must surely be obvious to us that the way of life and the values that they are recommending are just *obviously* rational and beneficial to us and to all reasonable folk. And we may thoughtlessly let that suggestion pass unchallenged. But in practice many or most moralities are far from being in any obvious sense either rational or economically or biologically efficient. For example, in Christian and Buddhist countries the institution of religious celibacy meant that for a millennium or more society devoted vast resources to attempting to ensure that intellectuals (literate people, the cleric/clerks, the monks) had no children. But why try to breed the brains out of the population? And in the same culture-areas throughout the same period there also flourished an aristocratic warrior-ethic through which societies regularly achieved the slaughter of large crops of their most vigorous younger men and the devastation of their lands and cities.

The celibate ethic and the warrior-ethic seem, both of them, to be very harmful to society and also, surely, hostile to each other. Yet both have enjoyed enormous prestige, sometimes in the same society at the same time. Why?

In his last books, Georges Bataille begins to develop an interesting answer. All societies, he suggests, need a way of burning off their surplus production, whether it be of young men, or bulls, or wealth or whatever. The excess may be devoted to warfare, or to the building of monasteries, or to bullfighting, or to feasting and the exchange of gifts. The institutions (war, monasteries, etc.) that carry out the destruction become very powerful and develop moralities of their own, and the ritual acts through which the destruction takes place give symbolic expression to their vision of the world.

We can now reformulate the doctrine that 'Every ethic dramatizes a metaphysic' as follows: many or most moralities, such as those of the warrior and the monk, were developed in connection with great social institutions like war and religion. Through these institutions society

38

destroyed its surplus in ways that ritually reflected and purged its sense of life and its vision of the world. Thus, it may seem that everything is transient, our life is brief, glorious and violent, and that the world is an arena in which conflicting forces struggle for ever. Warfare and a warrior-ethic may be one way of symbolizing and responding to this vision of the world; religious asceticism and the attempt by purifying one's immortal soul to gain a better world may be another.

Solar ethics is a third. It attempts to say an all-out religious Yes to life's pure transience. The human being is seen as a flowing process of self-exteriorization (German, *Sichäusserlichierung*). We must pour ourselves out into symbolic expression, in order to get into and play our part in the public social world. The 'broadcast' self (as one might call it) has a passion for self-expression. It really longs to realize itself by pouring itself out and passing away. In so doing it may gain, by a curiously negative and indirect route, a form of objective immortality. The voice and personality of the broadcaster the late Brian Redhead, for example, remain very vivid to millions of people in Britain precisely because he was so easy, going. The fact that he is now dead and gone makes us only the more aware of the sense in which his 'easy, going' lightness makes him live yet.

Solar ethics, you will have gathered, is highly extravertive. It says that we can realize ourselves, and 'live', only by the self-exteriorization, self-expression, self-communication through which we join the common world. Your soul is not behind but *in front of* your face, which is why your partner correctly claims to be able to 'read you like a book'. You can be read like a book because you give yourself away. We all do so; we have to do so.

Solar ethics turns us inside out. It does not make the traditional dualistic contrast between an inner mental world and an external physical world. Instead there is only one world, the world our language gives us, the world our language inducts us into. Your mind is your field of view, your angle on the world and the part you have to play in our common life: that is what 'fills your thoughts'.[1] Freeing us from a great many old illusions, solar ethics precipitates us into the one and only 'real' world, the world of our common language.

Note

[1] Idioms expressing the outwardness of mind are surprisingly many and strong. Imagine the form of words you might use to invite somebody to contribute to a debate: 'What's your view? How do things look from your standpoint? How do *you* see it?' And notice how in political commentary the very word 'perception' is nowadays often used to mean 'interpretation from a certain angle or perspective'.

7

Becoming Objective

A long tradition in our culture has suggested that the inward route is the best and shortest way to God. If you seek the Good, if you seek salvation, then you should recollect yourself and attend to the state of your soul. You should purify yourself and practise contemplation.

However, I am trying to move in exactly the opposite direction, arguing that we don't need to become subjective: we now need to become objective. That is, the only way to the Good and to salvation is by going out into symbolic expression. The human soul is not on the inside of the human being, but on the outside, for it is only in our objective symbolic self-expression that we succeed in making anything of ourselves. Only on our outsides do we make any sense at all. When we go to the theatre, we make psychological judgments about the characters in the play, just on the basis of observation of their outsides. And that is all we need. Nothing is missing. A human being is a highly socialized animal with cultural inscriptions written all over the surface of its body like tattoos, so that its behaviours — all the noises it makes, and the things it does — come out as legible motions of signs. (In this connexion, see for example such works of fiction as Ray Bradbury's *The Illustrated Man* and Jeanette Winterson's *Written on the Body*.) The result is that minds and meanings, soul and sense are culture-guided interpretations of goings-on not within, but on the *surface* of the human body. We don't *have* insides. In order to make any sense at all, we have to *do* things; we have to go out into symbolic expression and be read — by ourselves perhaps, and also by others. The only 'mind' you've got is the one that is just as readily accessible for other people to read as it is for you yourself to pronounce upon.

Accordingly I seek to replace the traditional ascetical ethic of withdrawal, solitude, self-examination, self-purification and self-control with a more Renaissance sort of ethic which pursues open publication, exhibition, declaration and show. Acknowledging that our late-capitalist media culture is increasingly a culture of public display, we should seek to put on a good performance, and make a brave show. By my dress even I make 'a fashion statement' (says M.H., jocularly, I suspect), and *a fortiori* you do so by yours.

The chief argument for the moral superiority of the extravertive way goes as follows:

1. A human being is, as it now seems, a biological organism; a complex moving self-maintaining system of energies, with many subsystems. Each subsystem has a part to play in maintaining the whole organism's life.

2. These subsystems have somewhat divergent aims; but they must all be active, and so they are all struggling for expression.

3. Human beings are social animals, who must co-operate with each other in order to survive.

4. Human beings must then communicate extensively with each other; and the symbol-systems they evolve must have the dual property of drawing conflicting forces within the self out into relatively-unified forms of expression which are at the same time functionally effective as messages. You've got to get it *both* off your chest *and* into his head.

So far, these first four steps in the argument are straight biology. They can be confirmed by, for example, observation of the courtship-behaviour of a bird, built up as it is out of components some aggressive, some submissive, and some borrowed from the tending and feeding of the young, and so on. That is the sort of language a prospective mate can understand, a synthesis of contrary elements. However, for strictly *philosophical* purposes 1-4 would need to be established, and can be established, by regressive analysis of texts or other human symbolic productions. Philosophy has to start from where it always is, namely inside language; so the present argument ought really to run *backwards*, from 6 to 1.

5. We humans, then, are *cultural* animals. We have to do so much communicating with each other, and must devote so much attention to reading each others' behaviours, that all our bodily expression has acquired potential symbolic meaning. Any and every bodily motion may perhaps turn out to be legible as body-language.

6. The sign as such, every sign, is in Freudian terms a compromise-formation. It resolves a conflict amongst the body-forces of the one who produces it. It lures conflicting forces within the self out into relatively-unified, coherent and efficient expression.

7. Thus it is that through symbolic expression we are able not only to talk to each other but also to pursue self-healing and personal integration.

8. Conclusion: conflict amongst the body-forces appears to be constitutive of our makeup, and perhaps no human being can expect ever to be wholly free from it. (Because they are genetically different from each other, there is even conflict between a pregnant woman and her unborn baby.) However, art in particular makes manifest the possibility of an objective redemption, our last consolation. And through art we may be led to see in the world itself our joint product and our objective redemption.

The account we give here differs a little from the doctrines to be found in Nietzsche and C. G. Jung. They both see the production of a body of creative work as being a way of writing one's spiritual autobiography in coded form. Nietzsche's psychic distress is in some way assuaged or relieved by creative work, and Jung more strongly sees creative artistic production as positively therapeutic. 'Symbols attract and transmute libido', he says, meaning that symbolic expression is cathartic. Hence 'art therapy': the works you produce are milestones along the road to recovery. But I am not claiming (as Jung presumably does) that by writing *Die Winterreise* Franz Schubert procures either therapy or even relief for his psychic distress and his grief. Perhaps he died as sad as ever, so that one cannot claim that through his music-writing he achieved anything much in the way of personal and subjective redemption. But if he loved music more even than himself, if he longed to express himself musically, and if he poured out his heart into his music, then he may be said to have won not subjective but objective redemption in and through his expression. The artwork becomes his objective redemption by what it does for *us*, rather than for him.

'Becoming objective' thus means, amongst other things, ceasing to care about one's personal fate. The novelist Jean Rhys says something of the sort about 'Writing': engaging with it did not actually *diminish* her extreme personal unhappiness, but at all times she knew that it was something more important than herself or any other individual. It was like a great ocean into which each individual writer wants to pour something, however small her contribution. And in France something similar has often been said about both *La peinture* and *L'écriture*.

This begins to make clear the very big difference between our ethical emotivism or expressivism and the older moral realism or objectivism. It is said, perhaps rightly, of some young men that they are too wayward and unstable to be able to cope with civilian life on their own. They really need to join the army, for such men can only flourish if they are held within a firm disciplinary framework. In civvy street they might end up criminals or vagrants, but the army gives them public standing, dignity. And they love the army for it; men like them are the best soldiers of all.

Such is moral realism, which in the West was generally defended against the background of the doctrine of Original Sin. A tradition going back through Kant to St Paul represents old-style moral realism as picturing the universe as a school, the Moral Law as the school rules, and human beings as scruffy schoolboys. But this metaphor is somewhat tendentious, for it reminds us that eventually we will leave school, and so implies that moral realism is only a temporary arrangement. It would be fairer to see moral realism as claiming that human social life will *always* need a fixed moral framework to give it stability and dignity. Without such a framework, society in the end breaks down.

Our ethical emotivism-expressivism is rather different. We say: moral realism just has died. Sorry about that; but it simply has happened. The entire vocabulary of the rational soul, conscience, the will, the moral law and so on is *dead*. The words are falling into disuse. It now appears that we humans are animals, social animals who must co-operate, but who find ourselves to be bundles of discordant impulses. To get ourselves together, and to procure enough co-operation for survival, we must go out into symbolic expression. So we must together generate the Symbolic Order, the so-called 'Ideal Culture' of language, religion, morality and art. The communally-generated Symbolic Order supplies each and all of us with forms of expression through which we can get ourselves together individually and socially, and conjure up our various visions of redemption. In art and religion we express our longing for satisfaction, wholeness, holiness, ideal beauty. But in these 'post-realist' times our expression has to be *solar* — which, be it understood, here means 'fully disinterested and objective'. One must be content to have produced an art-image, or a religious image, of a holiness and integration that will never become a finalized achievement. Solarity is a queer kind of post-sainthood, achieved only *in passing*, only in loss.

For there are no guarantees any more, and nothing that we

live by is objective in the old way. You may nevertheless turn out to be fortunate, and be able to obtain a happiness greater than anybody ever knew under the old realistic or objectivist dispensation. You may stumble upon a delirious eternal joy. But you have yourself to posit and love the ideal goodness and beauty that you serve and aspire after, in a purely disinterested and objective spirit, like Schubert's love of song, Cézanne's of *La peinture* and Jean Rhys's of Writing. There are no guarantees. There is no objectively-provided Reality, Goodness, Truth or Beauty any longer, at all. There's *nothing out there*. To that extent, nihilism has come and is henceforth our permanent human condition. That is so: it truly is so. You may nevertheless, as I say, enjoy such happiness and see such virtue as never existed under the old dispensation. But the reason why such an unprecedented and utterly amazing *excess* of aesthetic-ethical happiness is now possible, and may visit us, is that it is purely gratuitous and is available only on *solar* terms — that is, to those whose expression has become fully disinterested and objective.

Now you see why I have a bone to pick with Kierkegaard. Seeking to escape from Hegel's grandiose, totalizing — and sometimes irritatingly *abstract* — objectivism, Kierkegaard finds a way of undercutting it. He writes with the aim of leading his reader to see that there is a question that comes first of all, a question that logically precedes everything Hegel talks about and therefore undercuts Hegel's entire system, namely the question of my own relation to existence and my own infinite personal interest in my own eternal happiness. In fact, Kierkegaard's entire 'aesthetic' output of nineteen items, culminating in the *Postscript* of 1846, aims to bring about just one result: it seeks to heighten individual self-awareness, or inwardness — which means anxiety.

During that period the whole psychological sphere was being rapidly developed by writers such as Goethe, Stendhal and Coleridge. The concepts of melancholy, despair, dread, anxiety and *ennui* were relatively novel and attracting much interest. And anxiety is indeed at first sight very attractive. Pushing up one's own level of anxiety or brain-arousal heightens individual self-consciousness and considerably increases one's intelligence, analytical powers and productivity. It may also give one a gratifying sense of one's own superiority to lesser, slower and sleepier mortals. But the one thing that high anxiety can *not* be expected to deliver is long-term personal happiness. In the *Postscript* Kierkegaard writes like a demented spider, spinning out endlessly his line about becoming subjective, about subjectivity being truth — can *this* be the way to eternal happiness?

No, it quite obviously cannot. Kierkegaard winds himself and his readers up into a state of acute anxiety about the religious question — and then finds, inevitably, that he is stuck in that state, and cannot get out of it. 'Caught in his own web', says R.M. severely. What's he to do? In desperation, Kierkegaard tries to transfigure high anxiety *itself* into saving faith: 'the objective uncertainty held fast by the passion of inwardness'. But still the fact remains that you cannot hope to achieve a state of eternal happiness by way of working yourself into an anxiety-state about it. Anxiety, by a malicious irony, turns out in the end to be a dead end.

At this point then a central theme of Kierkegaard's teaching proves to be a mistake, and even a disaster. Hence, too late for me but perhaps not too late for you, I try to reverse him. We shouldn't seek to become subjective; we should seek to become objective. We should not withdraw into our own individual subjectivity, and we should not admire our own self-consciousness or our individual unicity. We should not cling in anxious attachment to our loves, our products or our expressions. On the contrary, we should simply expend ourselves and our lives, pouring ourselves out into expression and *immediately* letting go. One should not cling either to one's own selfhood or to anything that one has done, been, made or loved. One should live by repeated, continual, self-exteriorizing and self-shedding, self-expression and self-abandonment. Throwing away, forgetting oneself.

Kierkegaard was a protestant and a capitalist — or at least, the son of a capitalist — and he uses the familiar protestant-capitalist vocabulary of personal venture and gain, interest and saving. But I propose that we should reverse that vocabulary, thinking instead in terms of heedless prodigal self-expenditure. We should forget the self and its interest. We should see our life as a process of expression that is not attached to itself, but simply wastes itself: pours out and passes away. And my claim is that if along these lines we can become completely objective, ditching ourselves even as we express ourselves, then we may, we may, find a truly astonishing happiness being gratuitously superadded. But don't *bank* on it. It comes only unlooked-for. The only true way is the way of No Way.

Note

I should acknowledge a debt: the doctrine of self-shedding that I have here put forward was (I think) first suggested to me by Vivekananda. We should discard our *karma*, he says, claiming to be expounding the *Gita*. Both in Nietzsche and in Buddhism there is to be found a doctrine of liberation by forgetting. The truly magnanimous person does not brood over but simply forgets slights and injuries suffered, and temptations borne. See, for example, nos 3 and 14 in '101 Zen Stories'; in Paul Reps, *Zen Flesh, Zen Bones*, Penguin Books 1971: a temptation has been overcome when the original occasion of temptation has been quite forgotten.

8

Nihilism and Solarity

So we are solar because we are nihilists — is that the message? When we find that we have lost everything and don't believe anything any more, there is nothing left but solar for us to be. We are the only suns that still shine in an empty universe. Is that it?

No, that is not quite what we are saying. A certain misunderstanding here arises from the fact that nihilism is a scare-word left over from the late-nineteenth century. It was used, and perhaps still is used, to frighten the *bourgeoisie*, by which is meant that great mass of worthy folk who just assume that the best state of affairs is the one in which people are blessed with the most confidently realistic beliefs about God, about the moral order, and about the world. Such people demand an objectively-real God, an objective scale of values and moral order in the world, and an objectively law-governed and fully-formed Cosmos out there, ready-made to be our home. They demand that the Universe shall be a larger version of their own well-ordered homes, in which everything runs like clockwork and there are Rules of This Household printed on the tea-towels and posted up in the bathroom. They want, they really do want, a domestic universe with cosmic family values; and they are in some cases even today still determined to go on believing against all the evidence that we do actually have such a Universe.

Nietzsche's 'nihilism' in the 1880s may be seen in retrospect as a determined attempt finally to frighten such people out of their illusions. Given the way modern knowledge has developed, it should be clear to us all by now that it is we who have invented our natural science, our picture of the world and our various moral traditions and religious beliefs. It is we ourselves who have given all the orders, and have painted in all the colours. We always have done so, and in one way or another always will do so. We do and we must strive together to impose workable patterns upon the excessive and disorderly flux of experience. Thus we build our human knowledge; but today we recognize that our human knowledge is only a changing human contrivance, and we can no longer deceive ourselves or others into supposing that it is absolute knowledge.

So Nietzsche's 'nihilism', alarming though it sounded in its own day, now seems almost a sober doctrine, and not very different from our own constructivism and anti-realism. And in any case there are two major respects in which we need to qualify it.

In the first place, Nietzsche's use of 'nihilism' as a scare-word concedes too much to the bourgeois Christian. For it concedes the assumption that realistic belief in God, the moral order and the Cosmic order would indeed be a good thing to have, if only it were possible. And that I deny. Realism is spiritual slavery. The realist God of the churches, objective, transcendent, distinct from and in apposition to the believer, is a symbol of religious alienation. The more firmly such a God is believed in ('fundamentalism' being the extreme case) the more demonic and disastrously *ir*religious religion becomes; whereas in true religion people feel divine world-forming, value-conferring life welling up *in themselves* and flowing out through their own eyes and their fingertips.

Secondly, realistic belief in a moral Law, in a moral world-order, and in One True Morality out-there is similarly a symbol of moral alienation. It keeps human beings permanently fixated at a moral age of about 11 or 12 years, 'rigid' as the psychologists call it. Moral adulthood develops only as we gradually acquire the confidence first to break the rules, next to make new rules, and then to recognize that we ourselves always were the only legislators. We are not fully moral beings until we accept our own responsibility for creating the moral order.

And thirdly, the history of science shows that the order of the world does not exist out-there either. *We* invented our natural sciences and formulated our 'Laws of Nature', and we will ourselves in time come to recognize the limitations of their usefulness and their need of being reformulated or replaced. People who take a realistic view of physical law should be asked what it would be to find one of them, subsisting out-there. How would you identify it? What would it look like?

The same questions should then be asked about moral 'absolutes'. What would it be to find one of these remarkable objects? How would we be able to identify what it is: what would it look like? And if these peculiar objects, 'absolute values', really do exist objectively and independently of us, exactly how do they, merely by being there, get to twist our arms and pressure us to do this or that? What is the machinery by means of which they make us offers we cannot refuse?

In short, realism, whether of the scientific or of the moral or of the theological kind, can *itself* scarcely be understood realistically — just as literalism cannot itself be understood literally. Realism in practice is a form of rhetoric, used by some group of professionals to enhance their authority over us. The best response to it is to say, 'Well, you would say that, wouldn't you?' And if we all know in our hearts now that realism is just quackery, rhetoric, a confidence trick, then we ought not to need portentous talk about nihilism to break our attachment to it.

Which brings us to the second point: Nietzsche, the early Heidegger, Sartre and some others had a way of picturing the lonely human being as being *de trop*, adrift in an ice-cold barren universe, bereft of value, and finding himself stuck with the sole responsibility for creating and projecting out the values to live by. But this is never in fact the situation, for we always find ourselves in a world that is already fully appropriated by human beings and covered all over with our human values. We are always already within language, and within some historically-evolved human construction of the world. Everything is already theorized and evaluated.

Have you ever opened your eyes and seen great colourless blanks in your visual field? Of course you have not. There are no holes in the continuum of experience. The world is full, and every bit of it is recognizable. Every human being is always already within a complete, fully-formed and value-laden *human* construction of the world. *You would not, you could not be even yourself unless that not-self were already before you.* There is no human being who isn't already in a complete human world. You are, as they say, 'situated'.[1] Your world, around you now, is as essential to constitute you as what you are as your own body is. For not only do you define your world, but also your world also defines *you*: the self and the not-self always belong together, as any biography will show.

So we-and-our-language-in-our-world are always a complete, outsideless and yet in every way purely-contingent whole, in a manner which perhaps Wittgenstein, amongst all the canonical philosophers, came nearest to grasping.

So everything is contingent, everything is human and everything is ... *solar*! Solar.

Note

[1] For the notion of the 'situatedness' of human selfhood in Continental philosophy, see Sonja Kruks, *Situation and Human Existence*, Unwin Hyman 1990. Notice that 'situation' is roughly equivalent to my term 'objectivity'.

Students were intrigued by the statement that our world is always already complete. 'How is this so?' There are two traditional lines of reply. The first, from Kant's Transcendental Aesthetic, argues for example that we must think of space and time as being continuous, with no gaps in them. *A priori*, the world has to be thought of as a plenum, says Kant. The second argument is that, just as the horizon goes all the way round and has no end, so the great lines of distinction, that are drawn from top to bottom of the cosmos and from side to side, have no ends. The line that separates A from not-A cuts across, or goes around, the entire world. The great distinctions are endless, establishing language and world as outsideless but finite wholes. As all humans have to have language, so they always have a cosmology, and it is always a complete world-picture, just as every language is a complete language.

Let us take this one step further. There are no primitive and incompletely-made worlds for the same reason that there is no primitive and only half-developed language. Both 'language' and 'world' are entities such that they have to be complete, and *therefore just right for us*. Throughout all of history hitherto the contingent has been portrayed as utterly unsatisfactory on its own: the biggest single innovation of the present century has been the discovery of the outsideless completeness of the contingent realm. A truly wonderful discovery.

9

Solarity and Mortality

To become truly solar we need to become in the fullest sense
naturalized citizens, and that means citizens of this world
only, without any remaining trace of the old idea of dual
citizenship. That requires us to think of ourselves as being
transient and mortal all the way down, which is not an easy
thought to carry through consistently. No doubt the reason
for this is that in the past our denial of death has been so
many-stranded, and so deeply-engrained in the language.

We have, for example, believed in 'substance' as relatively
independent and self-identical being — an idea that is
already incipiently anti-temporal. We have gone on to claim
that the human self or soul is a substance, with the
implication that in some deep and inward respect we remain
self-identical and do not change because we already belong
to another and unchanging world. The passage of time may
erode away the body, the 'outer man', but deep down we like
to think the core-self is not suffering any erosion. Next, we
have an ancient convention that thinks and speaks of people
as becoming more fully-formed, more real and substantial,
bigger, more *set*, as they grow older. And finally we have a
large number of narratives and metaphors, applying both to
the individual and to the cosmos, which picture this life and
this time of struggle and change and development as leading
up to a blessed future time of perpetual, secure and
unchanging perfection and happiness. The metaphors speak
in terms of journey and destination, battle and victory, toil
and rest, shadow and substance, time and eternity, and so on:

and they all suggest that the point of life will eventually be revealed to us in a timeless realm after life. 'This' life is only preparatory, and our mortality is not truly constitutive. The body wears out like an old suit of clothes, but the real self goes on.

It is significant that the very way people speak of 'this' life, 'this' world, seems to whisper to us the suggestion that there is also another. But if we are ever to become fully naturalized citizens of 'this' world, we really do need to purge ourselves of such ideas. Our cosmological theory now pictures the world as being something like a slow-motion explosion. Everything is utterly transient; everything just pours out, spreads, scatters and passes away. There is no totalization and no final End to the process. 'Everything flows', as one of the first philosophers said, and so it is with us human beings too. We burn, burn up and burn out; the fire gradually sinks and dies down. We are grass, perishable.

Like it or not, the future will be naturalism in world-view and an ecohumanist ethic. We need sentences, text(ile)s, that will weave together into one continuous flowing process, pouring out and passing away, biology and language, flesh and word, *Natur* and *Geist*, the vibrating energies of the physical world and our own pulsating feelings. We need ways of writing the unity and continuity of the world — its continual coming to pass, and also its continual passing away. Me, I am sixty years old as I write, and I have less than twenty per cent of me left. I am a candle already well burnt-down. But the thinner I get, the more objective I become, and the more I love the world.

Objective? The Sun is objective, in the sense that its rays as such can't be seen. They become visible only 'objectively', that is, by falling upon some object and illuminating it. The Sun is nothing but its own self-outpouring and its own continual disappearance into objectivity as the world is lit up and enlivened by it. And we become steadily more objective, and blissfully so, as we get older, thinner, more emptied and outpoured, and so more lost in the objectivity of world-love. For this to work, we must be made of just the same stuff as the world. There is thus a very close connexion between mortality and objectivity; and now the argument can be taken a step further. We are our own transience, our own finite stretch of time and our own burning away. And because I am finite and woven without remainder into the process of the world, I now see that each individual's world is, for that individual, complete and exactly as long and as broad in scope as the extent of her own life. My world, the world I've had, is the objectivity of the life I've had. As the continental philosophers say, the self is always *situated*, always with and passing away into its world, its Other, its objectivity. Pause, think of it. My world, my mate, my Other, my 'oppo', my *Alter Ego*, the objective human, my counterpart and my consolation.

A biography, we noted above, is never merely a psychological analysis of a solitary individual. On the contrary, biography is always written along the interface between the subject and her or his world.

From what has been said, you will be able to see how sharply we must disagree with and reject Nietzsche's disparaging treatment of pity and compassion. Would he describe the Sun's shining as an expression of weakness or *ressentiment*? Solar ethics is based upon a radically and thoroughly naturalistic vision of the world. The human self is melted down into the flux of world-events. It trembles and vibrates like everything else and in sympathy with everything else. Like the Sun it pours itself out into expression, and passes away into objectivity. This pouring out and passing away is our happiness, our 'glory'. So, for once, Nietzsche is badly wrong.

10

Thinking the World of Him

Solar ethics is an unusually thoroughgoing form of ethical naturalism, and in many respects a deliberate reversal of our tradition. For example, where Kierkegaard has described the self as a process of becoming, we on the contrary take pleasure in seeing the self as a process of passing away. We are not becoming anything except our own objectivity; and we are not going anywhere but *everywhere*, into dissolution. Thus we melt the self down into the flux of world-events, in such a way as to find a new starting-point for ethics in the relation between the self and its own objectivity, the setting-in-life that it is always passing away into. In this way the knowledge that we really *are* mortal makes us love the world more intensely than human beings have ever previously believed possible. As we see it the human self is always situated, always burning, always going out into expression in its own life-world, its objective *Alter Ego*, its counterpart, its mate, its work.

Thus the human self is placed in its world in such a way that the-objectivity-of-myself, my world into which I am always passing away, is both me and not-me. It is, as the old idiom has it, 'the apple of my eye'; it is the first and foremost love-object, my own life and life-world, that in which my soul delights, and so close to me that it is that through which and in relation to which I see everything else. Naturally, the person who means most to me is a typical catalyst and symbol of all this. A man may speak of his wife as his better half, and more than that, his very life, the light of his eyes, his soul's darling. She is his own objectivity.

The solar idea of salvation is thus radically immanent. In various ways I seek in the not-self — in my life-world — objects of love and allegiance with the power to draw out my heart, and focus my expression. I have found salvation when I have found something that I can give my heart to. It draws me out into unified objective expression in such a way, and with such intensity and gladness, that I experience the highest love of life and the purest love of death as being simply identical. That *solar* identity of yearning for death, love of life, and gladness in expression is life's highest happiness and our final salvation. Burning to death, pouring out, spent, passing away.

What objects have the power to arouse us, galvanize us into activity, focus our energies, and draw us out into expression? It would be a mistake to become exclusively fixated upon one object only, and it turns out that in practice the things that enthuse us are many and various. They are a strange miscellany, but those objects which are not human persons are nevertheless often spoken of in personal metaphors. For a dandy, his objectivity is his own public self-presentation — his 'image', as it is often called nowadays. For a patriot, the fatherland, mother country, homeland. For many a man, the work to which — as his wife may complain — he is 'married'. For many a religious person, her heavenly Father, his Holy Mother, her divine Bridegroom and so forth. For every teacher, the brilliant pupil-child who is the apple of his eye and the dreamt-of future continuator of his work.

From a solar point of view it does not matter very much what happens to be the catalyst. 'Orthodoxy' is dead, and capital-T exclusive Truth is dead. All that matters is that each of us shall find some thing or things that can act as the catalyst, and through which we can come to experience the solar identity of living and dying that religion calls eternal life.

The catalyst is often spoken of in cosmological or even

solar terms: 'He thinks the world of you', people say. 'She thinks the sun shines out of ...' — but I need not complete the phrase. It made me laugh when I heard it recently: so coarse, so co(s)mically true.

Equally instructive are the metaphors of fire and burning. A great love makes one burn furiously — and why? Because it makes one *pass away* more quickly, it makes one unusually *ardent*, eloquent ... do you see? The poets' talk about love immortalizing us is nonsense. Love consumes us, makes us burn away more quickly, exposes us to the wind of pure temporality, hustles us rejoicing towards death. Interestingly, the experience of pure present-participle Be-ing, which Heidegger laments and says we moderns have utterly lost, is not an experience of timeless solid Reality, but the exact opposite. It is the experience of pure fleetingness as a consuming fire into which one plunges with joy. Like the tip of a lit cigarette, time's leading edge is cruelly hot.

Note

In discussion the question of meditation was raised. What does the solar meditator meditate upon? The answer, I think, is that the solar meditator looks closely at something moving, because to watch something moving is to *see* time and change. In the past, meditators often sought to become as still as possible in a completely motionless environment, as if they were trying to escape from temporality. Our aim should be the opposite. We should watch things *coming to pass*. What a beautiful phrase that is!

A student points out that in *Fear and Trembling* Isaac is described as being Abraham's 'world', which shows that Kierkegaard knew all about love.

The Way of No Way

Jiddu Krishnamurti, born in 1895, was discovered by the Theosophists while still a boy. They recognized in him the promised world-redeemer who would unite East and West in his own person. He would be Maitreya and Christ rolled into one.

For twenty years Krishnamurti went along with these claims and was groomed for his high office; but then in 1929 he repudiated them with the well-known declaration that 'Truth is a pathless land'. This meant that there is no fixed path, no technique and no magic formula by means of which people can find the blessedness they seek. We should free ourselves from the idea that there is some ready-made Answer out there, waiting to be found by us. There is no credal formula, no technique or Path, no institution or charismatic Person by cleaving to which we can find salvation.

Krishnamurti's own subsequent teaching (later echoed by Alan Watts) seems to have been a therapeutic and somewhat Buddhistic version of the Negative Way. What we humans need is not addition but subtraction. We should seek progressively to free ourselves from our illusions, from our chronic lust for intellectual and moral bondage, and from our desire to 'get somewhere'. We need to lose our errors, unlearning, unlearning all the way down, to where? — to where we already are. Happiness? — it is simply to give up the errors and illusions that are making us *un*happy.

Such was Krishnamurti's version of the way of No Way;

and it is interestingly like and unlike ours.

Like, in so far as we do agree with him that the development of historical and critical thinking since the Enlightenment has progressively, and now completely, dissolved away all the 'absolutes'. As we now see it, what cannot be questioned cannot be believed either. But after everything has been questioned, we see that there is no ready-made absolute truth or value, and no ready-made right Way of life. Everything is only-human and fallible, everything is contingent, everything is historically-evolved. We must no longer dream of salvation by finding the Right Answer, the magic formula; and we should certainly not suppose that some great institution is authorized to set up and manage a domineering Régime of Truth. We should no longer put up with the idea that somebody or other has the right to order us about merely because he wears a big hat.

Krishnamurti's account is *unlike* ours, however, because in the end he like so many other Eastern thinkers points us towards a state of wordless primal Bliss that lies outside language. Buddhist thought in particular has indeed recognized that the objective world that we seem to see is a world of our own construction, but we are told that it is a *mis*-construction. 'In comparison with what?', one wonders. Next, we are told to abandon, undo, relinquish our habitual world-building-by-language, and then by long meditation to slow down, even to arrest the very movement of thought. When we are completely still and language has stopped, the world is undone — and Void Bliss supervenes.

This is what the Western religious tradition calls 'quietism', and what Nietzsche calls 'passive nihilism'. We reject it. We stay with movement, with the human and with language, because on our view the purely-contingent human world, the world of language, is outsideless. There is no Nothingness. The visual field is outsideless, and the world of linguistic meaning is outsideless. So, where Krishnamurti, Watts and other interpreters of the Eastern tradition put meditation and

Empty extra-linguistic Bliss, I am putting solar living, a solar spirituality, and solar self-exteriorization into objectivity. Not empty bliss, but to die in active self-expending world-love, is our blessedness.

What I am saying differs somewhat, not only from Krishnamurti, but also from philosophical rationalism and from Nietzsche.

Rationalist philosophy demythologizes God into Objective Reason, the happiness of beholding the face of God into the satisfaction that our intellect finds in the contemplation of timeless and necessary truth, and the system of religious dogma into a system of *a priori* truths. Spinoza does all this most elegantly, but (much though we love him) on this particular point we don't agree with him at all. Spinoza's philosophy is simply the rational ghost of theology. It has lost theology's heart, which was always its flesh and blood appeal to our feelings and imagination, and in any case even on its own terms it is not nearly naturalistic enough. Genuine naturalism is not the doctrine that everything is necessary, but the doctrine that everything, really everything, is utterly contingent, fleeting and baseless. So, whereas Spinoza demythologizes everything down to Objective Reason (or God, or Nature), we demythologize everything down to the Universal Human (or Christ, or Nature) — the point being that our Objective Other, our world, is always a complete and fully humanly-appropriated world. It is a world in every part formed by our language and coloured by our human feelings, and therefore contingent all through, flesh all the way down.

In about 1962 John Kennedy declared that half the scientists who had ever lived were alive and working now: and indeed the colossal growth of scientific knowledge since 1945 is filling in the fine detail of the world to a degree barely imaginable in earlier times. The mapping of the entire human genome, now proceeding apace, is but one example. To look at it closely is to see how the scientific world-view has changed since the days of early modern physics. In Spinoza's day everything seemed to come down to a rather simple framework of mathematical laws around which the physical world was built; and Rationalism seemed the appropriate philosophical response. But today, when *we ourselves* are reflexively caught up in the dizzy complexities of our own evolutionary theory, our molecular biology and our neurosciences, radical humanism is the appropriate philosophical response. That involves a shift from God to Christ, from rationalism to humanism, and from universal necessity to universal contingency.

In this context it is not surprising that Nietzsche, along with his admiration, felt also that Spinoza was rather too chilly and solitary. Solar ethics is now revealed as a form of radical humanism. Forming our world, loving it, pouring ourselves out over it and passing away into it, we individual humans are finding our fulfilment by going out not into Objective Reason, but into the universal human.

Such is our ecohumanism. It differs significantly from Nietzsche's doctrine. We make the world friendly and human, but Nietzsche is much more heroic, masculinist, and concerned with projects for self-forging and world-mastery. (*Weltherrschaft*, 'religious lordship over the world', is a technical term in Albrecht Ritschl's theology: see *The Doctrine of Justification and Reconciliation*, Vol III, 1874; ET by H.R. Mackintosh and A.B. Macaulay, Edinburgh 1898, ²1902, pp.609ff.) But today none of us would wish to understand either self-mastery or world-mastery in the typical late-nineteenth-century sense of these terms. And I have said that the work by which we describe the world, appropriate it to ourselves, embellish and familiarize it, is also an act by which we site ourselves in the world as its fully naturalized citizens.

Note

The class discussed this question: did the Buddha *discover* the Noble Eightfold Path? Did he find it already marked out and waiting to be discovered by someone, or did he simply *invent* it? Did he himself make up the truths he taught?

It is curious that before the late-twentieth century nobody seems ever to have posed this question. We answer that teaching to the effect that there is no grand, metaphysical, saving capital-T Truth — teaching that in various ways is delivered by the Buddha, Nietzsche's Zarathustra, Krishnamurti and even this book — cannot itself be the Truth. It is only a fictioned, regulative, small-t truth.

Does any vicious paradox arise? Zarathustra *orders* his disciples *not* to obey him. 'Don't follow me; follow yourself!' he commands, and provided we all understand the paradox, no harm is done.

Levity

A tradition going back at least as far as St Paul makes a contrast between two different dispensations and forms of life, under the general labels 'Law' and 'Gospel'.

The Law is always perceived as having been laid down by a great and ancient Father, who may have been either human or divine. It has divided up the cosmos into different zones and complementary kinds of thing, and the human world into degrees of rank, merit and ritual purity or impurity. Then, everything having been duly put into its slot, appropriate rules for dealing with it have also been laid down. Henceforth, good and righteous conduct is defined as behaviour that respects and confirms the cosmological distinctions. You are acting well when you act in a way that acknowledges and ratifies the existing construction of the world.

The point here is very important, because people so often and so hastily assume that morality is a Good Thing. We should replace that assumption by a more careful formulation: under the Law 'good conduct' is, analytically, 'conduct that works to confirm the divinely and traditionally established and approved order of things'. In the language of tradition-based societies, good conduct is conduct that shows to each person and thing its due degree of respect.

By contrast, the Gospel was originally an attempt to relativize the existing construction of reality, and therefore an attempt to relativize the Law, its discriminations and its definition of what is good. Gospel ethics tries to live beyond the distinctions, and therefore to live purely affirmatively, without *ressentiment*, without differences of respect, without dividing, discriminating or excluding. It is an ethical style for an 'open' world that no longer has a fixed structure.

Such a purely affirmative ethic, not differentiating people according to their rank or merit, has rarely been taught or attempted within the Western tradition. Who is there? Perhaps Diogenes the Cynic, and perhaps Jesus, whose enemies acknowledged that he was no respecter of persons (Mark 12.14 etc.), and who seems to have taught that we should be solar as God is solar (Matthew 5.45; Luke 6.35). He was highly solar himself. Who else? Perhaps Francis, and perhaps certain figures on the wilder shores of Anabaptistry. But such figures are very rare. More usually, we find that male persons of great authority — Paul, Augustine, Luther — have interpreted Christianity as confirming the established divine order rather than as being an attempt to live beyond it. Thus the ethical teaching in the Pauline letters firmly reinstates the idea that different degrees of respect must be shown towards different classes of person.

The philosophers (perhaps rather surprisingly) have done somewhat better, for both Spinoza and Nietzsche did at least consider, and even try to live, a purely affirmative or solar type of ethic. The aim is to live without what Spinoza calls 'passive' or reactive feelings, and what Nietzsche calls '*ressentiment*'; and so to be, like the Sun, indiscriminately outgoing and generous. This is not exactly an orthodox ambition. Because realism, the Law and theism have in effect always been equated, the two philosophers who came nearest to attempting a genuinely affirmative, solar, Gospel ethic — were the two most notorious atheists. 'Atheism' is to side with the Son against the Father, and with the utopian dream against the solid reality of the divinely-established order.

All this shows very clearly that Christianity so far has always been a symbolic celebration of the triumph of the Old Man over the Young Man, and of the Law over the Gospel.

66

It has been, too, a triumph of established reality over visionary aspiration, and of gravity over levity. Religiousness has been equated with seriousness, stability and well-foundedness, and has been sharply contrasted with the sort of levity and heedlessness of which butterflies are the traditional emblem.

Can levity be revalued? Yes, it should be. In the older realistic ways of thinking the imagery was always of weight, anchorage and grounding. Contingent and fleeting events and existences were stabilized by being tied back to and grounded in the necessary and the eternal, in a way that applied also to the moral life: one felt constrained by objective moral necessitation. But suddenly in recent generations that backdrop, which used to give anchorage and stability to the worlds of being and value, has simply vanished. Only lightness is left to us nowadays, and we had better learn to live with it.

Illustrating the shift, I heard a mother indignantly rebuke her child: 'William!', she said, 'That was quite unnecessary!'. She was one of those who feel that we do right when we are guided all the time by a background awareness of what is objectively fitting and morally necessitated. William evidently did not share her view. 'But, Mother', he might have retorted, '*Everything* is quite unnecessary.' There is no longer, in the old sense, a subsistent objective and constraining reason for anything. Everything has become ultralight. Everything is superfluous. Much that we do now, we do just for the Hell of it.

The idioms of Hell have changed interestingly. When puritanism was an important cultural influence, people who were reprobates and predestined for damnation might be spoken of as *hell-bent*, a word that very clearly suggests blind, stiff-necked, obstinate and self-destructive perversity. But the newer idiom is very different. If we do something 'just for the Hell of it', we do it gratuitously, superfluously, in the spirit of conscious playfulness by which we now mark our awareness of being newly emancipated from the old heaviness and seriousness of life.

Can levity be *religious*? Yes, if it be understood as transcendence without ontology, playful, mobile and humorous. Buddhism cultivates it — especially Mahayana, and especially, perhaps, Zen. A Christian version of it, *die Fröliche Wissenschaft*, the joyful wisdom, will quite deliberately relativize, make sport with, reverse and sometimes *send up* established religious ideas and doctrinal themes. Indeed, when we learn to understand religious beliefs and symbols in a non-realistic way, we learn for the first time how to take them lightly — and so discover how to do many new things with them.

A metaphor for this: the writing of Oscar Wilde at his peak is as clear as spun glass. So clear that like an optical fibre it easily carries a host of different messages simultaneously. In his *Alice* books, Lewis Carroll achieved the same solar richness and lucidity. But as a clergyman he was hopelessly serious, poor man, and is remembered as the preacher of a particularly grim and dismal sermon against the sin of joking about God. But suppose that Lewis Carroll had written about God as well as he wrote the Alice books — now, that would be religious writing such as we in the West have hardly known yet.

Further Reading

Books about ethics that are well-written and imaginatively exciting are very few indeed. I list below just about everything that is in any way close to *Solar Ethics*, and that has benefitted me as I have been writing.

Plato's early and middle-period Dialogues, especially the *Symposium* and the *Republic*

St Matthew's Gospel, chs 5-7, together with Kierkegaard's late *Christian Discourses* on texts from the Sermon on the Mount — especially those on the birds and the lilies (Arbaugh and Arbaugh numbering, nos 26, 30, 32)

Spinoza's *Ethics*

Blake's lyric poetry

Dostoyevsky's *The Possessed* (= *The Devils*)

Nietzsche, complete

Georges Bataille's later works

Michel Foucault's last (posthumously-published) writings, a miscellany of interviews, papers and draft books about the formation and care of the self

Index

Aristotle, 10
Arnold, M., 12
Augustine, 2, 9, 28, 66
Ayer, A.J., 8

Bataille, G., 21f., 38, 69
Betjeman, J., 20
Blake, W., 69
Bradbury, R., 41
Buber, M., 3
Bucklow, Christopher, 1
Buddha, 30, 64

Carroll, Lewis, 68
Cézanne, P., 46
Coleridge, S.T., 46

Darwin, C., 26
Descartes, R., 31, 35
Diogenes, 66
Dostoyevsky, F., 69

Foucault, M., 7, 35, 69
Francis, 66

Galileo, 31
Goethe, J.W., 46

Hegel, G.W.F., 46
Heidegger, M., 25, 51, 59
Homer, 2
Hume, D., 24, 35

Jesus, 66 et passim
Jung, C.G., 43f.

Kant, I., 32ff., 45, 53
Kaufmann, W., 35
Kennedy, J.F., 62
Kierkegaard, S., 9, 32f., 46ff.,
    57, 59, 69
Krishnamurti, J., 60ff.
Kruks, S., 52

Lacan, J., 25
Land, N., 22
Levinas, E., 3
Luther, M., 66

Macaulay, A.B., 63
MacIntyre, A., 7
Mackintosh, H.R., 63
Macmurray, J., 12
Mahavira, 30
Mannheim, R., 25
Monet, C., 19
Moore, G.E., 7f.

Nietzsche, F., 3, 7, 19, 34f.,
    43, 48ff., 56, 61ff., 66, 69

Ovid, 2

Paul, 45, 65
Plato, 23ff., 28, 30f., 69

Rabinow, P., 35
Redhead, B., 39
Reps, P., 48
Rhys, J., 44, 46
Ritschl, A., 63
Russell, B., 7f.

Sartre, J.-P., 51
Schubert, F., 44, 46
Socrates, 7
Spinoza, 62ff., 66, 69
Stendhal, 46

Taylor, M.C., 22

Van Gogh, V., 19, 21, 27
Varro, M.T., 2
Vivekananda, 48

Watts, A., 60
Wellington, the Duke of, 34
Whorf, B., 25
Wilde, O., 68
Winterson, J., 41
Wittgenstein, L., 25

Printed in the United Kingdom
by Lightning Source UK Ltd.
103356UKS00002B/382-426